C is for College!
An ABC book on college access

By Shamelle & Neils Ribeiro-Yemofio
Illustrated by Cameron Wilson

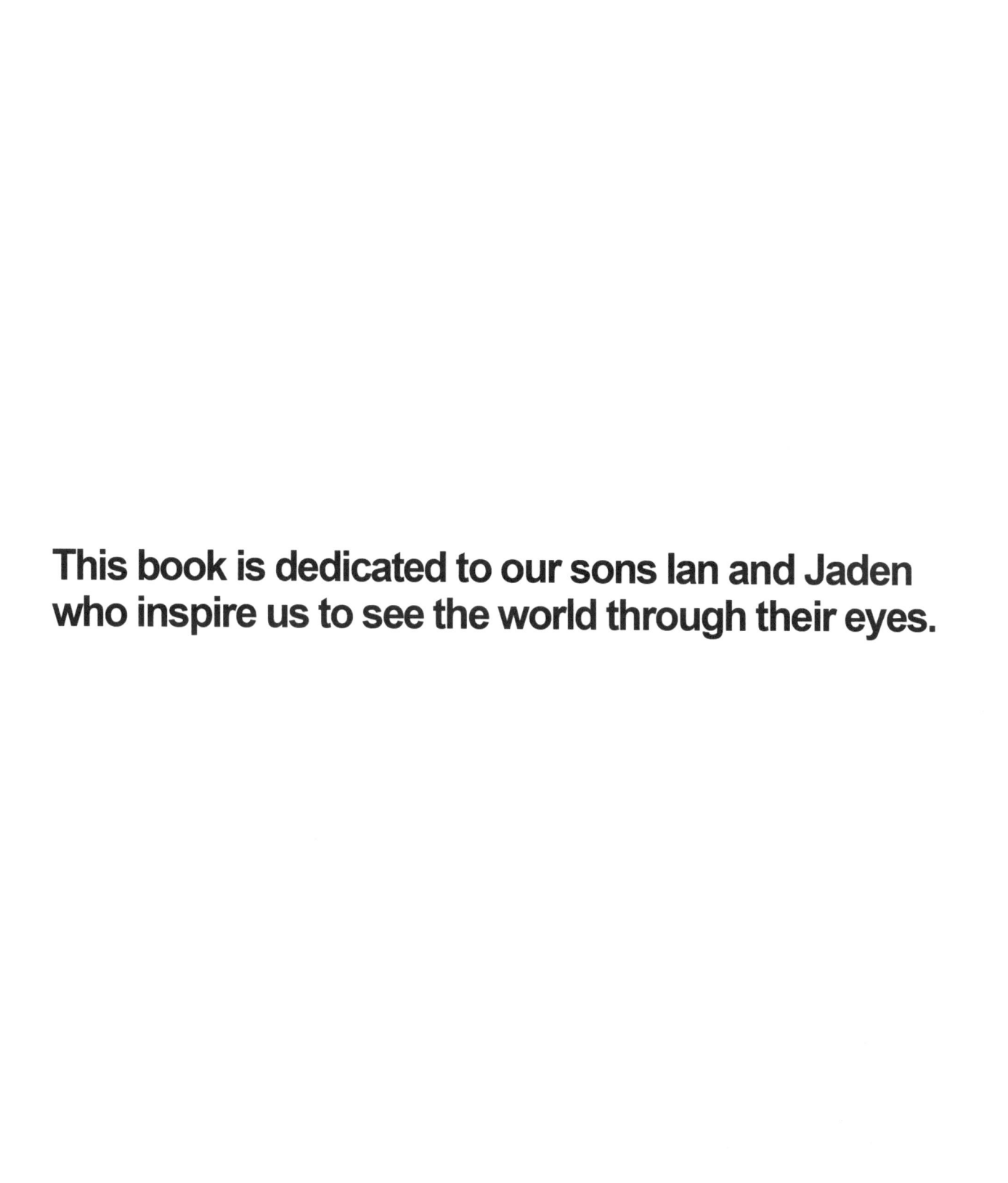

This book is dedicated to our sons Ian and Jaden who inspire us to see the world through their eyes.

First—preschool, elementary, and then there is middle—
the schools you attend from the time you are little.

You grow up still more, and high school begins.
Work hard, make friends, and graduate at the end.

But then, what's next? And what should you do?
Well then, find a college that's just right for you!

G - GPA (Grade Point Average)
In college all your work will earn a GPA.
Compute the scores in all your classes to find out your grade.

 **- Joining**
You'll often have fun in college when joining different things— a club, sorority, fraternity, or maybe a group that sings.

M - **Major**
"Oh, do you know what you want to be?"
is a question that you'll hear.
And carefully choosing a major
will help you plan your career.

 - **Office Hours**
If you need help from your professor beyond what's taught in class, then visit them during office hours, it may help you pass!

 - Quad
At college, there's often a place they sometimes call the Quad. A large and lawn-filled space to hang out with your squad.

S - Scholarships

And have you heard of scholarships? They're money to help pay for school. So get good grades and write essays 'cause earning money is cool!

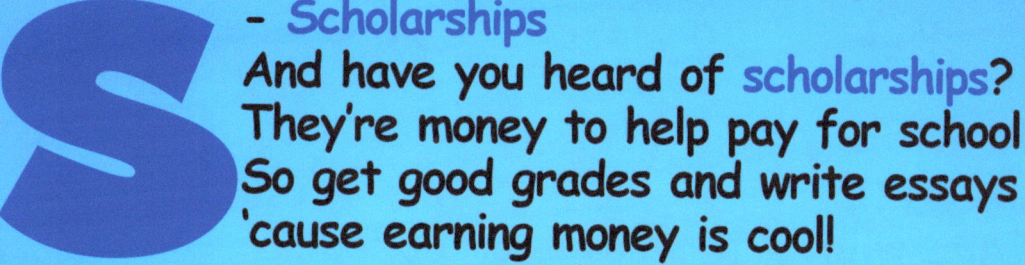

U - Union
A student union is the place where students often gather. A spot to study, where you can eat, or socialize if you'd rather.

 - Zz's

The college hours are packed with work—with sports, studying, and friends. Make sure to get a good night of Zzz's when each and every day ends.

CPSIA information can be obtained
at www.ICGtesting.com
Printed in the USA
LVHW071535030922
727557LV00015B/115